EP

DISCARDED

NASHVILLE PUBLIC LIBRARY

DISCARDED

In Nigeria
En Nigeria

written by **Judy Zocchi** illustrated by **Neale Brodie**

dingles&company New Jersey

For Mickey Aldorasi, Sr.

©2005 by Judith Mazzeo Zocchi

All rights reserved.
No part of this book may be reproduced in any form
without written permission from the publishers,
except by a reviewer who may quote brief passages
in a review to be printed in a newspaper or magazine.

First printing

PUBLISHED BY dingles&company
P.O. Box 508 • Sea Girt, New Jersey • 08750
WEBSITE: www.dingles.com • E-MAIL: info@dingles.com

Library of Congress Catalog Card No.: 2004095334
ISBN: 1-59646-011-3

Printed in the United States of America

ART DIRECTION & DESIGN BY Barbie Lambert
ENGLISH EDITED BY Andrea Curley
SPANISH EDITED BY Teresa Carbajal Ravet
RESEARCH AND ADDITIONAL COPY WRITTEN BY Robert Neal Kanner
EDUCATIONAL CONSULTANT Bridget Riley Turnbach
ART ASSISTANTS Erin Collity & Sara Sagliano
PRE-PRESS BY Pixel Graphics

The Global Adventures series takes children on an around-the-world exploration of a variety of fascinating countries. The series examines each country's history and physical features as well as its most popular customs, activities, and foods.

Judy Zocchi

is the author of the Global Adventures, Holiday Happenings, Click & Squeak's Computer Basics, and Paulie and Sasha series. She is a writer and lyricist who holds a bachelor's degree in fine arts/theater from Mount Saint Mary's College and a master's degree in educational theater from New York University. She lives in Manasquan, New Jersey, with her husband, David.

Neale Brodie

is a freelance illustrator who lives in Brighton, England, with his wife and young daughter. He is a self-taught artist, having received no formal education in illustration. As well as illustrating a number of children's books, he has worked as an animator in the computer games industry.

In Nigeria the NAIRA is what people spend.

Naira is the basic unit of currency of Nigeria. There are 100 kobo in 1 Naira.

En Nigeria el NAIRA es lo que la gente usa como moneda.

Naira es la unidad básica de dinero en Nigeria. Hay 100 kobo en 1 Naira.

The DUNDUN drum beats loud.

This drum is shaped like an hourglass. Sometimes the musician uses it to "talk" by imitating the tones of the Yoruba language.

El tambor DUNDUN pulsa fuerte.

Este tambor es en forma de un reloj de arena. Algunas veces los músicos lo usan para "hablar" por imitar los tonos del idioma Yoruba.

OIL is a major source of income.

Nigeria is one of the largest producers of oil and petroleum in the world.

PETRÓLEO es el recurso principal de ganancia.

Nigeria es uno de los productores más grandes de petróleo del mundo.

The ARGUNGU FISHING FESTIVAL always draws a crowd.

During this international fishing contest in the northern village of Argungu, fishermen rattle seed-filled gourds to drive fish to shallow water, then catch them with hand nets.

El FESTIVAL DE PESCA ARGUNGU siempre atrae el gentío.

Durante este concurso internacional de la pesca en la aldea del norte de Argungu, los pescadores hacen ruido con calabazas llenas de semillas para dirigir a los peces hacia agua somera, luego los atrapan con redes manuales.

In Nigeria DASH is a gift-giving custom.

In this culture, dash is an invitation to give something for which something is given in return.

En Nigeria el DASH es una costumbre de regalar regalos.

En esta cultura, dash es una invitación a regalar algo por cual algo más se regala a cambio.

AYO is an ancient board game people play.

This popular Yoruba game is played with seeds or stones on a board with hollow holes. The player who captures the most seeds wins.

AYO es un juego de tablero antiguo que la gente juega.

Este juego popular de Yoruba se juega con semillas o piedras en un tablero con huecos. El jugador quien captura la mayor parte de las semillas gana.

CAMELS with one hump are trained to race.

This is a popular sport in which jockeys race dromedary camels across the sand toward a finish line.

CAMELLOS con una giba están entrenados para las carreras.

Este es un deporte popular en el cual yoquis compiten en carreras de camellos dromedarios a través la arena hacia una línea de llegada.

Some **HOUSES** are made from earth and hay.

The walls of some Nigerian houses are made from tied bundles of hay and mud mortar.

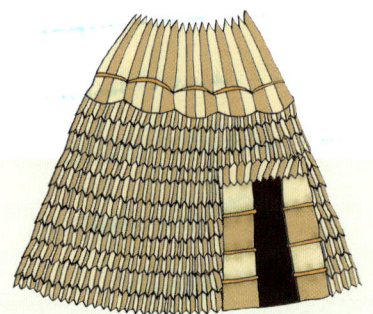

Algunas **CASAS** están hechas de tierra y heno.

Las paredes de algunas casas de Nigeria están hechas de bultos atados de heno y de mortero de barro.

In Nigeria a BUSH TAXI takes people around.

Bush taxis are used for public transportation. The seats are replaced with long benches to make room for more passengers.

En Nigeria el TAXI BUSH conduce a la gente.

Los taxis bush se usan para la transportación del público. Los asientos se sustituyen con bancos largos para hacer más espacio para más pasajeros.

PUFF-PUFFS
are doughnuts sold on the street.

These delicious treats are small balls of lightly sugared fried dough that look like doughnut holes.

PUFF-PUFFS son donas que se venden en la calle.

Estas golosinas deliciosas son bolas pequeñas de masa frita y azucaradas ligeramente que se parecen a las bolas de donas.

NOK sculptures are the earliest form of art.

One of the earliest known terra-cotta heads was found in Nok, a small village in northern Nigeria.

Esculturas NOK fueron la forma de arte más temprana.

Una de las cabezas de terracota primeramente conocida se encontro en Nok, una aldea pequeña del norte de Nigeria.

SNAILS are sold by the bucket to eat.

Snails are eaten regularly in rural areas of Nigeria. Snail meat is an inexpensive source of protein.

CARACOLES se venden en cubetas para comer.

Los caracoles regularmente se comen en áreas rurales de Nigeria. La carne del caracol es una fuente económica de proteína.

Nigerian culture is fun to learn.

La cultura nigeriana es divertida para aprender.

NAIRA
(NEH-ruh)

DUNDUN

OIL

ARGUNGU
(ar-GOON-goo)

DASH

AYO
(eye-oh)

CAMELS

HOUSES

BUSH TAXI

PUFF-PUFFS

NOK

SNAILS

OFFICIAL NAME:
Federal Republic of Nigeria

CAPITAL CITY:
Abuja

CURRENCY:
Naira

MAJOR LANGUAGES:
English, Hausa, Yoruba

BORDERS:
Gulf of Guinea,
Benin, Niger,
Chad, Cameroon

CONTINENT: Africa

ABOUT NIGERIA

The Nok people lived in the area known as Nigeria around 2,000 years ago. After them came the Kanuri, Hausa, and Fulani people. The Fulani Empire controlled the area from the beginning of the nineteenth century until the British took over in 1886. It officially became a colony of Great Britain in 1914 and gained its independence in 1960. It has been under military rule for much of the time since gaining its independence. The country has much internal strife as Muslims and Christians continue to fight one another. Nigeria is the most populous country in Africa. The country's chief resource and major industry is oil. Nigeria is known for its beautiful textiles and wood carvings.

UNDERSTANDING AND CELEBRATING CULTURAL DIFFERENCES

- What do you have in common with children from Nigeria?
- What things do you do differently from the children in Nigeria?
- What is your favorite new thing you learned about Nigeria?
- What unique thing about your culture would you like to share?

TRAVELING THROUGH NIGERIA

- In which region of the African continent is Nigeria located?
- Nigeria lies in one of the hottest parts of the world. How do you know this?
- What are the names of the two main rivers that run through Nigeria and meet at the Niger River delta?

TRY SOMETHING NEW...

Shake hands with your friends the Nigerian way! First, shake hands. Then, as you slide your hands back, click your thumb and middle finger together.

For more information on the Global Adventures series or to find activities that coordinate with it, explore our website at **www.dingles.com**.